feed their imagination

happy food
for happy children

To Izzy
and Oscar...
Eat up!

_____

To Mum, the
source of my
creativity... this
one is for you. x

happy food for happy children

mark northeast

absolute press  A.

First published in Great Britain in 2012
by Absolute Press, an imprint of
Bloomsbury Publishing Plc

Absolute Press
Scarborough House
29 James Street West
Bath BA1 2BT
Phone 44 (0) 1225 316013
Fax 44 (0) 1225 445836
E-mail info@absolutepress.co.uk
Website www.absolutepress.co.uk

Publisher Jon Croft
Commissioning Editor Meg Avent
Design Matt Inwood & Claire Siggery
Photography Matt Inwood
Editorial Assistant Andrea O'Connor

ISBN 9781408186923
Printed in China by C&C Printing Ltd.

A note about the text This book was set using
Cooper Black and Helvetica Neue. Cooper Black
was designed by Oswald Bruce Cooper and first
produced by Barnhart in 1922, and acquired in
1924 by the Schriftguß AG in Dresden. Helvetica
was designed in 1957 by Max Miedinger of the
Swiss-based Haas foundry. In the early 1980s,
Linotype redrew the entire Helvetica family. The
result was Helvetica Neue.

Bloomsbury Publishing Plc
50 Bedford Square, London WC1B 3DP
www.bloomsbury.com

funky
lunch

visit the
website:
www.funkylunch.com
or e-mail:
munch@funkylunch.com
or follow on Twitter:
@funkylunch
or join on Facebook

funky lunch

15 zoom, zoom, zoom! 17 chomp, chomp!
19 yo ho ho! 21 two scoops
23 fresh as a daisy 25 make it snappy!
27 creepy crawly 29 home sweet home
31 oink, oink! 33 baaaaaaaaaa!
35 an aquatic taste 37 all aboard!
39 twit twoo 41 flutter by 43 nessy
45 tall order 47 king of the jungle
49 happy birthday! 51 go bananas!
53 catch of the day 55 santa's little helper
57 great white bite 59 pretty polly
61 feline peckish? 63 hop to it!
65 tentacled treat 67 dairy delights
69 clowning around 71 crust-aceous lunch
73 out of this world 75 cock-a-doodle-do
77 sounds delicious 79 up in the clouds
81 take things slowly 83 down periscope

funky party

in the beginning...

'Don't play with your food!' was the usual response from my parents as I sat at the table as a child mindlessly pushing food around my plate in a daydream. I was a bit of a fussy eater and would turn my nose up at most things my mother put in front of me at meal times, especially if it contained 'greens'.

Fast-forward some 30 years, and as a parent I wondered if I too would experience such epic battles of defiance between a child and a plate of food. Luckily I was blessed with children who would try something at least once, but from experience I know that meal times are never straightforward in any household.

The idea for Funky Lunch started as a bit of fun, a way to cheer up a grumpy four-year-old who didn't want anything for lunch one day. I could have just let him go without, but decided to try and put a smile on his face and cut his sandwich into a space rocket shape. The result was an instant hit with a big smile and an empty plate.

Always up for a challenge, I decided to continue making these mini sandwich feasts on a regular basis. As I posted the results of my efforts online they soon became a talking point, with friends on Facebook asking what was coming next. So I set up a website for Funky Lunch displaying my 'works of art', and the media soon picked up on it. In a very short space of time, it became a global news story with people talking about Funky Lunch from as far afield as Brazil, China, Canada and Australia. Appearances on television made me realise just how much interest my creations had generated and parents worldwide emailed to say thank you for helping with their food dilemmas.

In the years since I made that first sandwich I have spoken to many people who have come to believe in what Funky Lunch set out to achieve ... happy food for happy children.

I feel very honoured having the opportunity to write these books and to work with the amazing people that have helped me. Yet at the same time I feel humbled that parents will want to buy them, to be inspired and create food for their children that will help them to enjoy new flavours or become part of a special day. I have no airs and graces, I'm not a cook by trade, I just love experimenting with food. I was discussing the journey that Funky Lunch has taken me on with a complete stranger recently and we were talking about writing the books and he said to me ... 'This sounds fantastic, so are you a chef then?' 'No,' I replied, 'I'm just a dad'.

get funky

Templates The simplest way to get started with your funky lunch is by creating a template. Take a piece of paper or card and draw out the shape of a slice of bread so you know how big your design will be. Once you have the 'frame' for your lunch you can draw the shape you need and cut it out. Place your template on to your bread and use a knife or scissors to create your sandwich shape. A selection of templates to get you started can be found online at www.funkylunch.com/templates.

Tools I want Funky Lunch to be something that everybody can try at home, something that in essence requires a minimum amount of utensils and can be adapted to be as simple or as extravagant as you like. This is why the main tools in my sandwich-making kit consist of a small sharp knife, a vegetable peeler, an apple corer and a few shaped cutters. You don't need to go out and buy equipment, just improvise... if you can't find anything to cut small circles with, just clean up a few felt-tip pen lids and use those instead. Plasticine cutters can also come in a variety of shapes and sizes so are ideal for cutting out the smaller details you may need from things like cheese and vegetables. With a jam jar, a pen lid and a milk bottle top, you should be able to make the face, eyes and nose for a character. From there, the possibilities are endless....

Ingredients We all know how hard it can be sometimes to get children to eat the things that are good for them and I make no guarantee that your little ones will suddenly start munching down on fruit and vegetables after seeing this book; but even if it just sparks an interest in different foods, then surely that's a start? Don't stick to my recipes... get creative! If you know that no matter how hard you try they'll never eat a tomato, swap it for some red pepper. If they loathe carrot, substitute some Red Leicester. Similarly, if you want to introduce your child to new flavours, what better distraction for them? I've tried to suggest alternative ingredients as we go, but you know your child best so give them what you think will grab their attention and make them want to try it.

Finally... Some of the recipes here take more time and effort than others. They're designed for all occasions from quick, midday snacks to party time treats. You should adapt them in whichever way suits you and come up with your own inventions. And when you have, send them through to me and I'll post the best ones on the website for everyone else to get funky with.... Enjoy!

munch@funkylunch.com

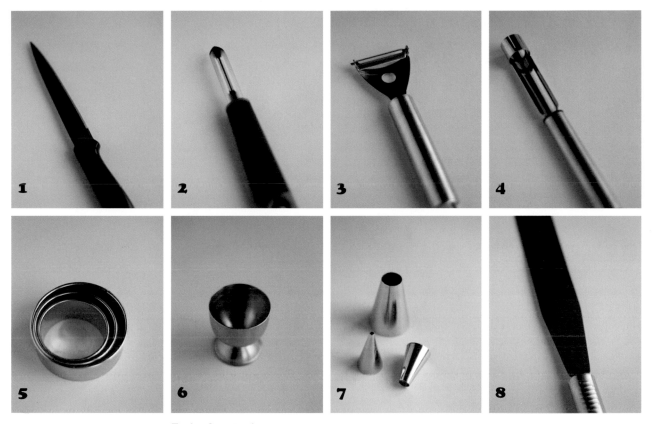

Tools of my trade
(1) a simple, sharp knife (2&3) vegetable peelers (4) apple corer (5,6&7) circle cutters...
in all shapes and sizes (8) a pallete knife – perfect for moving or flipping delicate things
(a fish slice is good too)

funky lunch

Meal times with children who are fussy about their food can be very stressful. And yet most of the time their reluctance to finish a meal comes down to simple boredom. Young minds need inspiring, so the concept for *funky lunch* was born out of the desire to turn an ordinary lunchtime sandwich into something a bit different – and a lot more exciting – in order to encourage children to eat a varied lunch that incorporated healthy ingredients in a fun way.

From my first space rocket sandwich onward I tried to make each new sandwich better than the last and something that would appeal to my children both visually and in terms of flavour. The range of designs soon burgeoned to include the Loch Ness Monster, a giraffe, a lion, a monkey, flowers, spiders, goldfish, houses – and even a sandwich 'birthday cake'.

But while trying to be as creative as possible, I did stick to a set of rules: every one was made using ingredients found easily in the fridge and each should contain as much fruit and vegetables as I could get into the design. There was one last rule, the most important for any sandwich to be considered a true success: it had to be eaten ... all of it. These rules continue to govern all the recipes in this book.

So whether you are trying to broaden your child's taste buds, struggling with a picky eater or you just want to put a smile on a grumpy four-year-old's face, I hope the ideas in this section will give you the inspiration to try something different, encourage better eating and feed their imagination.

zoom, zoom, zoom!

Blasting off from a lunch plate near you! A perfect little midday meal for the mini gastronaut in your life.

1 Assemble your sandwich using two slices of bread and your favourite filling.

2 Cut out the shape of the rocket with a sharp knife.

3 Carefully cut a square in the top layer of the bread and remove it for the window (the sandwich filling should show through). You can always fill this gap with a piece of ham, cheese or carrot.

4 Next, cut 2 'flame' shapes from a slice of carrot and top with a jagged piece of cheese to form the rocket booster.

5 Decorate your plate with some stars cut from cheese and a planet made from a slice of cucumber.

Try tomato or red pepper to give your rocket boosters a bit more crunch.

You will need   **bread   sandwich filling   carrot   cucumber   cheese**

chomp, chomp!

How many feet can you count as you munch your way through this little creation?

1 Make your sandwich using the bread and filling. The thicker you make the sandwich, the longer your caterpillar will appear in length.

2 Using a small circle cutter or egg cup, about 4cm across, cut as many circles from the sandwich as possible. Start in the corners to get the most from your bread and then arrange each circle of sandwich next to each other on their sides.

3 Cut 4 slices of cucumber about 5mm thick and then quarter each slice to give you 16 feet segments. Place 8 feet on each side of the body and trim down in size if they are too big.

4 Slice some cucumber lengthways and make 2 matchstick-size pieces for the antennae. Use a cocktail stick to make 2 holes on the top of the tomato and poke the antennae into the holes to hold them upright.

5 Using the remainder of the sliced cucumber and a small circle cutter, make 2 eyes and a half-moon-shaped mouth and stick these to the tomato face using the cream cheese. Finish off the eyes by sticking on small circles of grape skin.

As the sandwich pieces are standing on their side a filling such as cream cheese should help to hold them together and keep them in place.

Instead of cucumber feet and antennae, try carrot or celery for a sturdy substitute. You can also use cheese for the eyes and mouth.

You will need • bread • sandwich filling • cucumber • (good size) cherry tomato • red grape • cream cheese

yo ho ho!

Set sail on the high seas, *me hearty*, with this edible pirate adventure.

1 Assemble your sandwich using two slices of bread and your favourite filling.

2 Cut the shape of the ship's hull from your sandwich.

3 Take an apple corer and carefully make three portholes in the side of the ship's hull, removing just the top layer of bread.

4 Place the sandwich on a plate and use the breadsticks to form a mast and use the slice of ham for the sail.

5 Finish your sandwich with a skull-and-crossbones flag made from cucumber and cheese and then set it to sail on a sea of cucumber slices.

A sea of lettuce leaves makes a great alternative to cucumber.

Instead of a ham sail, use a slice of cheese for a meat-free alternative.

You will need • bread • sandwich filling • bread sticks • ham • cucumber • cheese

two scoops

Who says you can't give them ice cream for lunch? Just make sure they finish this one first!

1 Assemble your favourite sandwich using one slice of normal bread and a crust and cut this into the shape of an ice-cream cone.

2 Make another sandwich and with a small cup or cookie cutter, cut two circles from the sandwich.

3 Using the same sized cutter, cut a circle out of the cheese and a circle out of the ham too.

4 To assemble your ice-cream, place the ham slice on top of one of the sandwich circles and the cheese slice onto the other sandwich circle. Then position the two circles above the cone-shaped sandwich on your plate.

5 Finish it off by cutting a slice of cucumber to stick in the top.

For mint choc-chip ice cream, try using slices of green apple with the skin on, decorated with raisins.

You can use a slice of wholemeal bread for the cone if they won't eat the crust.

You will need • bread • crust of bread • sandwich filling • cheese • ham • cucumber

fresh as a daisy

Bring a little flower power to lunchtimes by serving up this blooming marvellous sandwich.

1 Make two sandwiches using your favourite fillings.

2 Using a cup or cookie cutter as big as you can fit on your sandwich and cut both into large circles.

3 With an apple corer, cut out a small circle from the centre of each sandwich but only remove the top layer of bread.

4 To make the petals for each flower, work around the sandwich making thin v-shaped cuts and removing the excess. Do this six or seven times until you have worked around each sandwich circle.

5 Take a cherry tomato and carefully remove the skin with a sharp knife in one piece. Now roll up this thin strip of tomato skin and place it into the centre of the sandwich, allowing it to loosely unroll a little.

6 For the stalks and leaves of your flowers, remove a strip of cucumber skin using a potato peeler and then carefully cut this into thin strips and place below your flowers.

7 Take some slices of cucumber and cut a few leaf shapes out and place at the bottom of the stalks along with a strip of cucumber skin cut into pointed blades of grass down one side.

Make cutting easier by using a clean pair of scissors, rather than a knife, to make the grass and leaf shapes.

Thin slices of spring onion or chives are a good alternative for the stems and grass.

You will need • bread • sandwich filling • cherry tomato • cucumber • cheese or carrot

make it snappy!

Get used to your little ones ordering *croc-monsieurs* from now on....

1 The crocodile is made by cutting two separate shapes from one sandwich and joining them together. Make your sandwich and cut it in half from top to bottom, then with the first half cut the body and head shape (it should resemble a stretched-out snowman). Cut out the long, curved tail section from the other sandwich half, ensuring the widest end of the tail section matches the width of the base of the body section.

2 Arrange both sandwich pieces on a plate and using a peeler to remove some skin from a cucumber, lay it down the length of the crocodile from head to tail until it is covered. Use a pair of clean scissors to trim the cucumber to match the body shape.

3 For the teeth, cut a wedge from the skinned cucumber and taper it at one end (this will form the back of the mouth).

4 Trim the other end to match the shape of the mouth and then use a small sharp knife to cut carefully across and through the cucumber at angles to form teeth. Remove the excess cucumber to leave you with an open mouth and sharp-looking teeth.

5 Open up the sandwich at the head end and insert the cucumber teeth between the two slices. You may need to trim some cucumber off the top and bottom of the mouth to make it fit without tearing the bread.

6 To make the eyes cut semi-circular wedges of cheese or cucumber and finish with cucumber skin pupils.

7 Finally, cut a slice of cucumber about 1cm thick and then quarter it. Use these quarters and carve some toes to make the feet.

Swap cucumber skin for thin slices of celery to give your croc some crunchy scales.

If cutting the teeth seems too tricky, use small triangles of cucumber or apple to fill up the mouth.

You will need • bread • sandwich filling • cucumber • cheese
(The crocodile shape is a bit tricky, but you can download a template from the Funky Lunch website. See page 8 for details.)

creepy crawly

They'll be taking more
than just incy-wincy bites
out of this lunchtime treat.

1 Slice open and make
up the roll using your
favourite filling.

2 Take a sharp knife
and gently cut a
shallow big smiling
mouth shape into
the top of the roll and
remove just the crust.

3 Spread your cream
cheese into the
mouth area and
smooth it out to
leave some big white teeth.
You can use thin strips of
cucumber skin to define
the lines between the teeth.

4 Cut two circles
from a slice of
cheese and
top with two halves
of black grape to make the
eyes.

5 A spider would not
be a spider without
his legs, so using
cucumber skin
again, cut eight legs and
tuck them into position
underneath the roll.

Instead
of cheese
and grape eyes,
try cucumber
and olive
instead.

If you
don't want
to use a roll,
just cut a
sandwich into
a circle.

You will need • wholemeal roll • sandwich filling • cheese • cream cheese
• black grapes • cucumber

home sweet home

Plate one of these up for lunch and encourage them to eat you out of house and home.

1 Make the sandwich using 2 slices of bread and your filling and then cut it into a basic house shape.

2 Cut the crust into a triangular roof shape and place it on top of the house. Make a chimney stack from the leftover crust and cut at an angle to match the slope of the roof.

3 Take a slice of cheese and cut it into three equal-sized small squares for the windows.

4 Slice three sides off a cherry tomato and then cut each slice in half. Trim the six pieces of tomato down until they match the size of your windows and then shape one side in a curve to finish the curtains.

5 Remove a large section of cucumber skin and trim it into a rectangle to make the front door.

6 With the leftover cucumber skin, cut 6 thin strips to mark out the window panes.

7 Finish with a few flowers cut from cheese, tomato and cucumber and a couple of roughly torn pieces of bread can be used for chimney smoke.

Use flower-shaped pastry or plasticine cutters to decorate the plate.

Use square slices of apple for the windows and pepper slices for the front door.

You will need • wholemeal bread (slices and crust) • sandwich filling • cheese • cherry tomato • cucumber

oink, oink!

Stave off the big bad wolf of hunger by serving up these cute little piggies for their lunch.

1 Before making your sandwich, take a large circular cookie cutter and cut a big circle from one slice of bread for the body. Using a smaller cutter, make another circle for the head. Use butter and sandwich filling to stick these two pieces together.

2 From the leftover bread cut two small ears and a smaller oval shape for the snout. Cut the same oval shape from a piece of ham to and lay it on top the oval of bread. Cut two pieces of ham to fit the shape of the ears.

3 To make the nostrils, push two holes right through the ham and bread of the snout using a small cutter or chopstick.

4 To layer up your sandwich, first place some cucumber skin beneath where the nostrils go and then place your bread and ham nose back over the top. You should then be able to see the dark cucumber skin through the nostril holes.

5 Finish your sandwich by making some eyes from discs of cheese and cucumber and finish with a twist of carrot for the tail.

Raisins make a great alternative for their miniature eyes.

To get a perfect curly tail, soak a strip of carrot in cold water for a few minutes and then wrap around a pencil and leave for a few minutes longer.

You will need • bread • sandwich filling • ham • cheese • cucumber • carrot

baaaaaaaaa!

These scrummy sheep should help ensure your flock are eating and not bleating at the lunch table.

1 Make your sandwich using the wholemeal bread cutting a tapered rectangle with one end rounded for the nose and cut two small semi-circles for the ears.

2 Next, cut a cloud shape for the top of his woolly head from the slice of white bread.

3 Using a small circle cutter, gently make 2 holes in the nose. Then cut 2 same sized circles from a slice of cucumber skin and push these into the nose holes on the bread.

4 From a slice of cheese, make 2 oval eyes and then finish with 2 small circles of cucumber skin.

Replace cucumber nose and eyes with green pepper or grapes.

Instead of using bread for the hair and ears, why not try using a slice of cheese cut to shape.

You will need • **wholemeal bread** • **50/50 white bread** • **sandwich filling** • **cucumber** • **cheese**

an aquatic taste

These sweet little sea creatures should enchant even the most stubborn of appetites.

1 Make your sandwich and then, using a sharp knife, carefully cut out the head, body and tail shape of your mermaid in one piece.

2 Lay the cheese slice on the top half of her body and trim round the shape with a knife or clean scissors.

3 To make the hair, use the darker orange cheese and cut around the outside of her head to match the face slice and then, using a sharp knife, gently carve out the hairline around her face as in the picture. Place some strands of shredded carrot on top.

4 Peel some skin from a cucumber and use it to make the scales on her tail.

5 Finish your mermaid with some small slices of grape for her bikini top and small cucumber eyes and mouth.

Make the rocks by using half an apple topped with halved grapes.

If you can't find any orange cheese, just use more strands of carrot for the hair.

You will need • bread • sandwich filling • cheese slice • orange cheese (red leicester's perfect) • carrot • red grapes • cucumber

all aboard!

Sit back and watch them chew-chew their way through this little train.

1 Make your train sandwich using the brown bread and filling and then use a sharp knife to cut out a simple train shape.

2 Take one of the offcut lengths of crust and place it along the bottom of the train.

3 Carefully cut away and remove an area of the top slice of bread to create a window.

4 Cut 3 round slices of cucumber and trim them down if necessary to use for the wheels. Tuck them in between the sandwich slices so just over half a circle is showing.

5 Remove some long strips of cucumber skin using a potato peeler and then, using a sharp knife, cut the skin into long thin strips and use it to give the train some markings around the engine and funnel.

6 You can finish by laying down some cucumber tracks, a carrot for the dome on top and some fluffy clouds of steam from the slice of white bread.

Turn this sandwich into a long party platter by making lots of carriage sandwiches and attaching them onto one another in a long line.

You will need • bread • sandwich filling • cucumber • cheese • carrot

twit twoo

They'll have a hoot eating this wide-eyed, feathery feast.

1 Make your favourite sandwich using the filling of your choice and then cut it into an oval shape – a bit like an egg.

2 From the top layer of the sandwich, cut a small oval shape, starting from the bottom of the owl's body, to just over halfway up. Gently remove this top layer of bread and then, using your slice of white bread, cut a shape to match the piece you have just removed.

3 Place the white bread oval into the gap on the sandwich and then, using a small knife or cocktail stick, scratch around the join of the white bread and brown to merge the two pieces together so it looks like a feathered edge.

4 To make the eyes, cut the outline of a number 8 and turn it on its side. Finish the eyes with two small circles of cucumber skin.

5 From a thin slice of carrot, cut a triangle shape and rest this in place for the beak.

6 The feet can be cut from a small wedge of carrot and then cut small V-shapes to form the claws.

7 Decorate your plate with a breadstick tree branch and then sit your owl onto the plate in position.

Try using two slices of hard-boiled egg for the eyes as the white and yellow make a perfect base for your wide-eyed owl.

You will need • wholemeal bread • 50/50 white bread • sandwich filling • cheese • carrot • cucumber • breadstick

flutter by

A nicer species of butterflies for the tummy! These ones should allow their hunger to take flight pronto.

1 Cut out the shape of a butterfly from your prepared sandwich.

2 To make the body, use a slice of cheese and cut it into a pencil shape with a point at one end and a round head at the other.

3 Using thin strips of cucumber skin you can give your butterfly a stripy body, smiling face and antennae.

4 Now get your assortment of tomato, carrot, pepper and cucumber pieces and decorate your butterfly to your own design.

Instead of vegetable decorations, use red and green apple slices, grapes, blueberries and more for a special fruity twist.

Give your child the basic sandwich shape and a selection of colourful vegetables and let them create their own patterns, eating as they go.

You will need • bread • sandwich filling • cheese • tomato • pepper • carrot • cucumber

nessy

Perfect for putting to rest the rumbling bellies of little monsters.

1 Slice your bagel in half and prepare it using your favourite filling (cream cheese helps to hold it all together well).

2 Cut your bagel in half to give you two semi-circles and place one on its side to form the back of the monster.

3 Taking the other half of the bagel, cut it into two and round off one end for the head. Cut the other piece into a pointed tail, still using the curve of the bagel for the shape.

4 Make a small hole in the side of the sea monster's head and fill it with cream cheese and a small cucumber skin circle for the eye. Perforate the front of the head with two holes and put a tiny round of cucumber skin into each for the nostrils. Use a knife to cut a slit into the bottom of the head and then fill with a slice of cucumber (skin side outwards) to form a mouth.

5 Remove some slices of skin from a cucumber and cut about twelve triangle shapes from them. Tuck these shapes in between the bagel slices to form the spikes along his back.

Stabilise the head by 'cementing' the pieces to the plate with cream cheese or propping it up with a cocktail stick (remove the stick before you serve).

You will need • bagels (as perfectly round as possible) • bagel filling • cucumber • cream cheese

tall order

Make sure their lunch is head and shoulders above the rest, with this cute giraffe.

1 Make your sandwich using two slices of bread and your favourite filling, and then cut out the giraffe head shape.

2 Take a third slice of bread, cut an oval shape to form the giraffe's nose area and with the leftover bread, cut a long rectangle to use as the neck.

3 Before putting the nose in place, make two holes using an apple corer for nostrils and place some thin strips of cucumber skin underneath the holes on top of the main sandwich.

4 Take your crust and cut the shape of the forehead at one end and with the remainder, cut out two horns and some circles of different sizes and place on the neck.

5 Give your giraffe some eyes and a mouth made from cucumber skin.

Use a slice of brown bread for the giraffe features, instead of the crust.

Black grapes or olives make a simple alternative for the eyes and nose.

king of the jungle

Rooaarring on to their plates, this beast of a feast will keep your wild ones full until teatime.

1 Assemble your sandwich using the slices of bread and filling.

2 Cut out the head shape from the sandwich and then use a piece of the leftover bread to form a triangle shape for a nose.

3 For the eyes, use oval-shaped pieces of sliced cucumber and finish each eye with half a black grape.

4 Take a slice of cucumber skin and mirror the shape of the bread nose as you cut, then lay over the top. Use a thin slice of cucumber skin to make the mouth.

5 For the lion's mane, take some slices of cheese and some carrot sliced lengthways and make lots of triangle shapes. Tuck these shapes in between the layers of sandwich, alternating between cheese and carrot to get a good mix of colour.

Avoid your bread drying out by cutting all of your triangles of carrot and cheese before you begin making your sandwich.

You will need • bread • sandwich filling • cheese • carrot • cucumber • black grapes

happy birthday!

Ensure many happy returns to the lunch table by serving up these impressive little cakes.

1 Make two sandwiches using the bread and your favourite fillings.

2 Cut each sandwich into a circle using a large cookie cutter or cup.

3 Cut the carrot into four sticks about 5cm long by 5mm wide and then cut a small section out of one end to make the candles.

4 Take a slice of cheese and cut four small flames and slot them into the top of the candles.

5 Place the two sandwiches on top of each other and then decorate around the base using halves of cherry tomato or grapes. Cut the birthday numbers you need from a slice of cucumber skin.

Make a large platter of little cakes and serve them as party nibbles.

Use a mix of white and red grapes or cherry tomatoes for decoration.

You will need • bread • sandwich filling • cheese • carrot • cucumber • cherry tomatoes or grapes

go bananas!

A wholesome treat for the little monkeys in your life.

1 Make your sandwich using your favourite filling and the bread.

2 Turn the sandwich so the crust is facing up and then cut out the shape of the monkey's head.

3 To make the face and ear sections, cut carefully into the crust and remove the top layer of the crust only, without cutting all the way through the slice.

4 Once the top layer of crust has been removed, make two eyes from small ovals of cheese and cucumber skin.

5 Finish your monkey by using more cucumber skin for the nostrils and smiling mouth.

Decorate the plate with pieces of banana to give it a fruity flavour.

It might be easier to make the sandwich with 2 slices of wholemeal bread and then cut an oval from a crust and place it on top of the nose area.

You will need • bread (including crust) • sandwich filling • cheese • cucumber

catch of the day

A fishy treat to reel in and eat!

1. Make your fishy sandwich using the bread and filling.

2. Cut it into an oval shape, slightly tapered at one end.

3. Take a carrot and, using a peeler, make long strips of carrot that will cover the body.

4. Starting at the head, place two strips of carrot next to each other in a vertical direction and leave a small gap and then another two strips of carrot and then leave a bigger gap before finishing with one more strip and a small gap at the tail end.

5. Using a pair of clean scissors, trim off any excess carrot that over-hangs the edge of the fish body.

6. Use three smaller strips of carrot with round edges and tuck them between the sandwich layers to form a tail. Using the same idea, make three rounded fins and tuck into place.

7. Cut the white part from a couple of cucumber slices to make two over-lapping eyes. Cut the pupils from cucumber skin and cut a small strip of cucumber for the mouth.

8. Finish your fish by accentuating the white stripes of the body with thin borders of cucumber skin.

Decorate the plate with a few bubbles made from thin circles of cucumber.

You will need • bread • sandwich filling • carrot • cucumber • rocket or lettuce leaves

santa's little helper

This festive feast uses toasted antlers to give Rudolph a touch of added crunch.

1 Make your sandwich using your favourite filling and two slices of bread, and then cut out the head shape.

2 From a third slice of bread, cut out a letter 'B' shape and place on its side at the bottom end of the head, place a small slice of cucumber skin in between

for the mouth. Cut two petal shapes from the leftover bread to make his ears and then two smaller-sized petals from the crust part of the bread for the inner ear detail.

3 To make the antlers, toast another slice of bread and then cut out two jagged shapes and position at the top of the head.

4 Create two eyes from circles of cheese and place half a black grape on each one.

5 Finish off your reindeer with a trademark red nose, made from a cherry tomato.

Be daring! Try black olives for the eyes instead of grapes.

Instead of a big juicy tomato nose, try a radish or a circular cut of red pepper.

You will need • brown bread • filling • cherry tomato • cheese • black grapes • cucumber

great white bite

Let your little sea urchins dive in and sink their jaws into these great white shark sandwiches!

 Make your sandwich and then cut the head of your shark out of the bread so it looks like a triangle with round edges.

 Take the leftover cuts of bread and make 3 fins and a tail from a single layer of the bread and put them in place on your plate.

3 To make the shark's mouth, cut the top layer and remove the bread to form an opening.

4 From two strips of cucumber or cheese, cut and remove small triangles leaving you with a row of sharp teeth.

5 Lift the top layer of bread and place a strip of cucumber skin on top of the sandwich filling where the mouth opening will be and then place the two rows of teeth on top. Replace the bread layer making sure the teeth and dark background can be seen through the opening.

6 Finish your shark with two menacing eyes made from cheese and cucumber and two tiny cucumber nostrils will complete this underwater treat.

Add a few jellyfish, made from thinly sliced halves of cucumber and strips of carrot.

You will need • bread • sandwich filling • cucumber • cheese

pretty polly

Let them get their beaks into these colourful characters and help keep them quiet for a while!

1 Make your sandwich using your favourite ingredients and cut out the shape of your parrot. You could use a hand drawn template to help you.

2 Cut some thin slices of cucumber lengthways and lay these on top of your sandwich. Trim the cucumber so it matches the outline of your bread.

3 To make the feathery wings, use wide thin slices of cheese, carrot and cucumber skin and give each piece a zig-zag end making sure that you stagger each slice as you layer them up.

4 Using a slice of carrot from the widest part, trim it to match the shape of the head.

5 Cut a small piece of cheese for the beak and then add some cucumber eyes.

6 The parrot's claws are cut from a thick chunk of carrot, leaving enough room to fit a breadstick perch in place.

Serve your parrot sandwich with a bowl of nuts, seeds or rasins to nibble on.

You will need • bread • sandwich filling • cheese • carrot • cucumber

feline peckish?

These little kitten sandwiches really are the cat's whiskers.

1 Make your sandwich using your favourite filling and then cut out an oval shape with two pointed ears for the head.

2 Peel off some lengths of cucumber skin and cut 6 thin strips and poke into the bread to hold the whiskers in place.

3 Cut 2 small eyes from cucumber skin and make the nose from circles of cucumber and cheese. Make the mouth from a piece of cucumber skin cut into a curved '3' shape.

4 Finally, cut 2 triangles of ham and place one inside each of the ear shapes.

Thin slices of spring onion are also perfect for a smart set of whiskers.

For a treat without meat, replace the little pink ham ears with red apple.

You will need • bread • sandwich filling • cucumber • cheese • ham

hop to it!

Indulge in a little midday magic by pulling this rabbit out of your lunchtime hat.

 Make your rabbit sandwich using two slices of bread and the filling and cut out an oval shape for the head.

2 Take a third slice of bread and cut out the ear shapes and place them into position on the plate.

3 Make two eyes by cutting oval shapes from a slice of cheese. Add pupils by cutting smaller oval shapes from cucumber skin.

4 Cut a small circular slice of tomato for the nose and use a piece of cucumber skin for the mouth.

5 Make the rabbit's teeth by cutting a small slice of cheese into two rectangles.

Decorate the plate with mini carrots by cutting wedges of carrot and using cucumber skin for the carrot tops.

You will need • **bread** • **sandwich filling** • **cucumber** • **cheese** • **tomato** • **carrot**

tentacled treat

Arm yourself more than
adequately for lunch with
this under-the-sea
spectacular sandwich.

1 Use your favourite
filling and two slices
of bread to make
your sandwich. Then
from it cut the octopus
head and the two front
tentacles in one piece.

2 Take another slice
of bread and cut
6 more tentacle
shapes and place
them behind the front two
on each side.

3 Slice the skin off
some tomatoes and
use a smaller
circular cutter to
make approximately
twelve small circles or
semi-circles. Place these
little 'suckers' onto the
tentacles, trimming the
tomato to make them fit.

4 Make the eyes,
eyebrows and
mouth from the
skin and flesh of
some cucumber.

5 Decorate your plate
with a sea bed made
from cheese and
lettuce leaf
seaweed.

When
layering the
tentacles, squash
a couple of them
down flat so they
appear to be
behind the ones
in front.

You will need • bread • sandwich filling • tomato • cucumber • cheese • lettuce

dairy delights

Your little herd will be over the moo-oon grazing over these.

1 Before making the sandwich, place 2 wholemeal slices of bread together and cut out the shape of the head excluding the ears.

2 With the top slice of wholemeal, cut away the centre section leaving 2 side areas for the eyes.

3 Cut a slice of white bread to fit on the head with a narrow section in the middle to allow the sides to fit on.

4 Using the leftover white bread, cut the outline of a number '8' for the nose and then cut two ears from the leftover brown bread.

5 To assemble, butter your bottom layer of bread and place the sandwich filling on top, then butter and place the main white section and the two brown sides into position.

6 Turn the nose section on its side and make two holes in each side and fill with small pieces of cucumber skin to look like nostrils and put into place.

7 Make two eyes using cucumber flesh, with skin for the pupils and finally tuck a small piece of ham underneath the nose-shaped piece of bread for the tongue.

Cheese and grapes make a tasty alternative for the eyes.

Instead of ham for the tongue you could use a pink piece of apple skin.

You will need • white and brown bread • sandwich filling • cucumber • ham

c owning a ound

Put on a big lunchtime performance with these bright and cheery little clowns.

1 Make your sandwich and cut it into a round or oval face shape.

2 Make the eyes using a disc of cheese cut into oval shapes and then use a small circular cutter to make two discs of cucumber skin for the pupils.

3 Take a large round cutter and from a wide slice of cheese cut out a circle. Take a slightly smaller cutter and cut another circle out of the middle of the first. Cut the remaining ring of cheese in half and round the edges off to make a big smiling mouth.

4 Grate a large carrot and bunch up the strands on each side of the clown's head. Cut two slices of carrot and score each with a knife to shape into bushy eyebrows.

5 Place the cherry tomato into the centre of your clown's face and then compose the other parts around it.

6 Finish the sandwich by laying two triangular chunks of cucumber alongside one circular chunk of cucumber to form a bow tie. Finally, add a very thin sliver of cucumber skin to make a smile.

Before eating, have fun trying different hair styles using the grated carrot.

Try using yellow pepper or big slices of red or green apple to make his bow tie.

sandwich filling   carrot   cheese   cucumber   cherry tomato

crust-aceous lunch

Perfect for the little nippers in the family.

1 Before making your pitta bread sandwich, cut the shape of the crabs body being careful to save both leftover side pieces.

2 Gently open your pitta and fill with your favourite ingredients.

3 Using the leftover pitta bread, cut out two oval shapes and then cut a zig-zag down the middle of each one; pull open at this cut to show off his big claws.

4 Slice 6 thick lengths of cucumber skin and cut each one into a curved point.

5 Arrange the 6 cucumber legs and two pitta claws on a plate and then place the crab's body over the top.

6 From a slice of cheese, make two eyes and a mouth, then finish with cucumber eyebrows and black grape pupils.

Pitta bread suits the crab's shape well, but you could use either a roll or sliced bread instead.

For a fruitier creature, swap the cheese eyes and mouth for slices of apple.

You will need · pitta bread · sandwich filling · cheese · cucumber · black grapes

out of this world

They'll need taste buds from another planet to refuse this extraterrestrial treat.

1 Make your sandwich using your favourite filling and then cut a large circle as big as you can get from your bread.

2 Gently, cut a smiling mouth out of the top layer of the sandwich. Then take two slices of cheese, cutting squares into the edge of each slice for a row of teeth. Cut a length of cucumber skin to the same size as the mouth. Carefully slide the skin and then, on top, the two rows of teeth inbetween the bread layers so as to show through the cavity made for the mouth.

3 To make the eyes, cut three small thin strips of cucumber skin and arrange in place, then using a small cutter or clean pen lid, cut three small circles of cucumber flesh and three circles of cucumber skin.

4 Slice off a piece of cherry tomato and decorate with three nostril holes.

5 Make the arms and legs by slicing some strips of carrot lengthways and then cutting into shape.

6 Decorate your plate with a cheese moon and some cheese stars too if you have a cutter to hand.

You don't have to stop at three eyes, let your alien imagination run wild.

Use a black grape for the nose if tomatoes are not a favourite.

You will need • bread • sandwich filling • cheese • cucumber • cherry tomato • carrot

cock-a-doodle-do

Another farmyard favourite guaranteed to have them clucking for more.

1 Assemble your sandwich using the bread and fillings and then cut a shape that is rounded at the top and has a zigzag pattern at the other end.

2 Using a small circular cutter, make two circles from a slice of cheese to form the eyes. Finish these off with two smaller circles of cucumber skin.

3 Take another slice of cheese and carefully cut the beak out to match the picture, removing a centre piece for the open mouth.

4 Before laying the cheese beak on to the sandwich, remove some cucumber skin and lay this into place first and then rest the beak on top. Make sure that the cucumber skin can be seen through the hole in the mouth.

5 Take a sharp knife and slice a thick layer of skin from a tomato. Press flat on a chopping board and then cut the tomato into a teardrop shape. Repeat this three more times and arrange three red 'feathers' on top of the head.

6 Place the last tomato feather on its chin and use some thin strips of cucumber skin for eyebrows and nostrils to finish.

You may find it easier to cut the tomato shapes with a small clean pair of scissors, instead of a sharp knife.

If your tomato is too squashy, use some red pepper instead for the feathers, as this will add crunch and be easier to cut.

You will need • bread • sandwich filling • cheese slices • cherry tomatoes • cucumber

sounds delicious

Give your little maestros a standing ovation, for finishing this tuneful treat.

1 The outline of the piano has two straight edges – one on the left and one across the bottom and a curved step shape that starts in the top left and goes down to the bottom right. Before making your sandwich, place both slices of bread together and cut out the piano shape.

2 Using the top slice of bread, cut along the bottom edge a strip about 1cm wide and remove. This is where the keys will sit. Cut a similar sized section from the same edge so that you are left with the curved lid and a strip of bread.

3 Butter and lay your filling on the other slice of bread, leaving room at the bottom straight edge to place a strip of cheese for the keyboard. Butter and stick the thin strip of bread behind the keys.

4 Cut three rectangular chunks of carrot into sturdy legs and place flat on a plate. Now rest the bottom layer of sandwich carefully on top of the legs so that it is sitting in position.

5 Using a thin stick of carrot, gently balance the small curved lid at an angle on top of the bottom slice.

6 To make the keys, press the tip of a cocktail stick into the strip of cheese to form small grooves and then with very thin slices of cucumber skin, cut small rectangles for the black keys.

Try using sticks of cucumber or celery to prop up your piano top.

The cheese and cucumber keyboard can be made in advance before placing it on the piano.

You will need • **bread** • **filling** • **cheese** • **cucumber** • **carrot**
(The shape of the body of the piano is a bit tricky, but you can download a template from the Funky Lunch website. See page 8 for details.)

up in the clouds

A colourful treat for when you're stuck inside on a blustery day.

1 Before making your sandwich, place a slice of white bread and a slice of brown together and cut out a diamond shape for your kite. Cut each slice across the width and length of the shape and then swap the top and bottom slices of bread around in one half of the top section and do the same in the opposite half of the bottom section, so you end up with a pattern that looks like ours.

2 Use butter and filling to make the four sections of sandwich and then place each section into position on your plate.

3 Cut some small thin rectangular slices of carrot and then trim each piece into a bow shape. Do the same with a slice of cheese so you end up with approximately 7 carrot bows and 5 cheese bows.

4 Remove a long thin slice of cucumber skin and cut it into a long strip to make the tail and then place five of each bow along its length.

5 Cut two more ribbon pieces of cucumber skin and attach these to the middle of the kite along with two thin strips of carrot topped with the final two carrot bows.

6 Finally, attach two more lengths of carrot ribbon to the base of the kite and then decorate your plate with a little cloud in the sky made from roughly torn white bread.

Chives or thin spring onions make good substitute ribbons.

Let them decorate the kite's tail using their favourite fruit or vegetables.

You will need • brown and white bread • filling • cheese • cucumber • carrot

take things slowly

A lunchtime treat for your little gastro-pods. This great sandwich idea was created by Funky follower, Theresa Croyle from Forest Lake, Minnesota, USA.

1 Slice open your bagel and pack it with a sandwich filling that will hold it together once upright.

2 Trim the wide end of a celery stick at an angle to form the head and cut the tail end of it to your desired length.

3 Cut a 'V' shape into one of the edges on the bagel so it sits nicely along your celery stick.

4 Using the offcuts of celery, make two thin sticks and fix them into the 'head' end of the celery by cutting a small slit each side and pushing them in place.

5 To make the eyes, cut a black grape in half and, using a small circular cutter, remove the middle of the grape and replace with a small circle of cheese, topped with a spot of grape skin for the pupil.

6 Using a small pointed knife, make a hole in the bottom of the grape eye and push this on top of the celery stick.

7 Decorate your snail's shell with thin strips of spring onion held in place with either butter or cream cheese.

For a genuine (albeit grisly!) touch, spread a trail of snail 'slime' behind your snail using a squirt of relish.

Dress your plate with lettuce leaves to get a real garden feel.

You will need • bagel • filling • celery • grapes • spring onion • cheese

down periscope

Dive, dive, dive into lunchtime with this underwater adventure on a plate.

1 Slice your roll lengthways and fill with your favourite ingredients.

2 Using a small circular cutter, make three porthole shapes down one side of the roll and remove the bread and any filling.

3 With the same sized cutter, make 3 circular windows from a slice of cheese and a thin strip of cucumber skin around the edge.

4 To make the submarine's periscope, cut a chunky 'L' shape from a piece of carrot and then round off the edges. Scoop out the end and push a small circle of cucumber skin into place.

If you can't find a sub roll then a hot dog roll will make a good alternative.

Fill the portholes with something already to size such as grapes or a slice of radish.

You will need • sub roll • filling • carrot • cheese • cucumber

funky party

As a child, my siblings and I were taught to appreciate the things we received and the birthday parties in our house were no different to those of other children growing up in the late seventies and early eighties. Of all the usual party food at the table – the crisps, the jelly and the sandwiches – the one thing that could always be guaranteed was a great looking birthday cake.

Mum's hobby was decorating cakes and throughout my younger years I was probably told on more than one occasion to 'step away from the table' as Mum delicately placed petal after intricate petal on to the most exquisite looking wedding and birthday cakes. I remember making my first character cake with Mum for our primary school fête. She helped make the chocolate sponge and then I carefully cut out a shape resembling ET the Extra-Terrestrial. I remember the pride of seeing it on display in the school hall with a '3rd Place' rosette next to it. My very first cake. I was nine years old.

Inspired by my childhood memories and my experience with creating Funky Lunches, this book is designed to help parents through the party process, to give them some fun but simple ideas to brighten up a table of food.

While the Funky Lunches in the first part of this book include lots of healthy ingredients and encourage children to try new foods, what sort of children's party doesn't have chocolate, jelly and other sugary delights – so they are in there along with the healthy food. We've tried to include ideas to cater for parties of all shapes and sizes, whether it is a small gathering at home, a large group of classmates in the village hall or a couple of friends round for afternoon tea.

ladybird toasts

Exceedingly cute tomato-and-olive toasts.

makes 12 toasts

4 slices of wholemeal bread,
    toasted
low-fat cream cheese
Little Gem lettuce
6 baby plum tomatoes
small jar of black olives

Spread a thin layer of cream cheese on one side of each toasted slice of bread and then press down the lettuce leaves on top so they stick to and cover the bread.

Use a small circular or flower-shaped cookie cutter to cut out three shapes from each slice of bread and set aside.

To make each ladybird, take a baby plum tomato and cut it lengthways in half. Get a black olive and cut this in half to form the head. Trim the tomato and olives so they fit together snug on the lettuce leaf circle.

For the ladybird spots, cut some small circles of olive skin with a clean pen top or small cutter (press hard for a clean cut). Use two small dots of cream cheese for the eyes.

funk it up...

• If you are making a large number of these, you can speed things up, whizzing a load of olives to a smooth paste in a food processor. Then use a piping bag to squeeze dots of olive mixture on to the ladybirds back.
• You can also pipe the cream cheese for the eyes.
• Why not see what other insects you can make from a few similar ingredients?

'x' marks the spot

Fun pancakes for your little treasures.

makes approximately 16 pancakes

170g plain flour
pinch of salt
3 eggs
400ml milk
40g butter, melted
vegetable oil
to decorate
strawberries
dark chocolate, melted
  (or chocolate spread)

Mix the flour and salt together in a large bowl and then make a well in the centre and crack in the eggs.

Beat the eggs into the flour with a whisk and gradually beat in the milk to get a smooth liquid the same consistency as single cream.

Leave to stand for 15 minutes and when you are ready to cook, whisk through the melted butter.

Heat a little vegetable oil in a non-stick frying pan until hot, and pour in a ladleful of the batter mixture turning the pan quickly to evenly coat the base. Cook for between 30 seconds and a minute until the base is lightly browned.

Use a palette knife to gently flip the pancake over and cook on the other side for a few seconds until lightly browned. Slide the pancake onto a warm plate and repeat the process with the remaining batter.

To create your treasure map, cut a couple of thin slices of strawberry to make your 'X' and then take some melted dark chocolate in a piping bag and pipe some random dotted line paths all over the map leading to the treasure.

Finish off by piping a skull and crossbones and then placing some strawberry stalks as palm trees around the map.

birthday 'cakes'

Sweet looking sandwiches.

makes 12 sandwiches

white and brown bread
variety of sandwich fillings
to decorate
low-fat cream cheese
carrot
sweetcorn
red pepper
extras
paper cupcake cases
cup cake stand

Make up six standard sandwiches using the bread and fillings and then using a small round cookie cutter or egg cup, cut out four circles from each sandwich.

Stick two mini sandwiches on top of each other with cream cheese and place into a cup cake case and chill to keep fresh.

To prepare your cake toppings, cut twelve sticks of carrot about 4cm long and 5mm wide and then take some cheese slices, cut the same number of candle flames.

Using the red pepper, sweetcorn and any leftover carrot, either finely dice or use some small shaped cutters to create little vegetable shapes like hearts, diamonds, circles and flowers.

To assemble your cup cake sandwiches, spread an even layer of cream cheese across the top of each sandwich.

Decorate the top of each sandwich by cutting a small section from the top of each carrot candle and slotting a cheese flame into each. Make a hole in the top of each sandwich to stand the candle in position.

You can now decorate the rest of each sandwich using the small segments and shapes of pepper, sweetcorn and carrot.

Arrange the cupcake sandwiches on a stand or plate and use as the centrepiece for your party table.

monster burgers

A devilishly good snack.

feeds 6

1 small red onion, finely chopped
2 slices of wholemeal bread
   (crusts removed)
250g/9oz beef mince
1/2 tsp of thyme leaves
sunflower oil
6 mini hamburger buns
   (or small soft rolls)
to decorate
red pepper
cucumber or olives
cheddar cheese slices

Sauté the onion in 1 tablespoon of oil for 5 minutes until it is soft. Tear the bread into small pieces and put it into a food processor with the onion mixture and whizz together.

Combine the mince, thyme and onion mixture in a bowl and then divide into 6 equal portions. Roll each portion in a ball and then flatten into a burger shape.

Fry the burgers gently over a medium heat for about 4–5 minutes each side until cooked through. Alternatively, cook them under a preheated grill.

While your burgers are cooking, prepare the decoration by cutting two triangles of red pepper for horns and two circles of cucumber or olive for the eyes. Push the horns and eyes into the top half of the burger bun.

To make the teeth, cut a slice of cheese into a large circle and then around one edge cut a zigzag pattern

When your burgers are ready, place them on to the bun base and lay the cheese slice on top just off centre so the teeth hang over the edge of the burger. The heat of the burger will slowly melt the teeth and bend them downwards.

Finish it off with a blood thirsty drizzle of ketchup oozing from the mouth.

funk it up...

Why not create a different looking monster burger for each party guest by using different styles of horns and eyes.

almost eggstinct

They'll have a cracking adventure with these little dinosaur eggs.

makes 6–12 eggs

6 small eggs or 12 quail's eggs
  (to make them bite-sized)
half a shredded red cabbage
3 slice wholemeal bread
lettuce leaf, for decoration

Place the eggs in a saucepan with the shredded cabbage. You may need to do this in two batches to fit them all in.

Fill the pan with water until it just covers the eggs and then bring to a simmer and boil for 7 minutes. Once boiled, remove the eggs from the pan and cool under cold water.

Gently tap the eggs to create small cracks all over the shell and then return to the coloured water and leave for 2 hours.

To make the nest, gently cut your slices of bread into thin sticks of varying lengths and arrange on a baking tray.

Pre-heat the grill and then place the baking tray under the grill and toast the bread pieces. Keep a close eye on them to prevent burning and shake them halfway through to ensure they are toasted on all sides. Remove when golden brown.

Arrange your toasted bread in a bowl or on a plate in a random nest shape.

When your eggs have soaked for at least 2 hours, remove from the water and either place in the nest unpeeled or remove the shell to reveal your colourful patterned dinosaur eggs.

funk it up...

You can add a little bit of food colouring to the pan to vary the colours and make them more vivid.

nocturn-owls

These scotch eggs are a hoot.

makes 8 owls

4 small eggs
275g/10oz sausage meat
1 spring onion, finely chopped
1 tsp chopped fresh parsley
1 tsp thyme leaves
125g/4oz plain flour, seasoned
1 egg, beaten
125g/4oz breadcrumbs
oil for frying

to decorate

cucumber or black olives
cheese
orange pepper or carrot

Place the eggs in a saucepan of cold water, bring to the boil and then simmer for 9 minutes. Drain and cool under cold water, then peel.

Mix the sausage meat with the herbs and spring onion in a bowl and then season. Divide the mixture into four balls and flatten into a large oval shape about 5mm thick. Put the seasoned flour on a plate and roll each egg in it to cover and then place into the sausage meat and wrap around. Make sure the meat covers the egg completely and has a smooth surface.

Dip each sausage-covered egg into the beaten egg mixture coating it completely and then roll in the breadcrumbs to cover all over.

Heat some oil in a deep pan until a breadcrumb sizzles and turns brown when dropped in. Carefully place the Scotch egg into the hot oil and fry for 8–10 minutes until crisp and golden and the sausage meat is completely cooked.

Carefully remove and drain on kitchen paper and allow to cool.

Using a sharp knife cut the Scotch egg completely in half lengthways and set aside.

To decorate your owls, cut two small circles of cucumber skin or olive for the eyes and fill with a circle of cheese and an even smaller dot of cucumber skin for the pupils. Use a slice of carrot or orange pepper, and cut a triangle shape for the beak. Arrange your owls on a plate using some toasted bread or chopsticks for tree branches and a crescent moon shape slice of cheese.

funky smoothie

Lip-smackingly good refreshment.

makes 1 smoothie

handful of strawberries
banana
splash of 100% apple juice
squeeze of lime juice
to decorate
red grapes
bendy black straws
1 strawberry

Place the strawberries, banana, apple juice and lime juice into a blender and blend until smooth. If it is too thick, add a little more apple juice. Pour into a tall thin glass.

To create the lips, take your strawberry, remove the stalk and cut a small 'V' shape into the top. Round off the bottom section of the strawberry to finish the shape of the lips and then cut another 'V' shape across the front of the strawberry for the open mouth. Cut a small curved slit in the bottom of your strawberry and slide it over the lip of the glass.

Extend and bend two black straws and then with the drinking end, trim the straw to 1cm from the bend. Take a grape and cut about 1cm from the non-stalk end. Push the shortened drinking end of the straw through the grape and out the other side. You may need to blow down the straw to remove the piece of grape stuck in there. Repeat with the other straw so you have a pair of eyes.

Trim the other end of the straws so that when placed in the glass, the grape eyes just sit on top of the strawberry lips.

crudités towers

Tea-time toppling!

500g of carrots
dips of your choice, to serve

Cut the carrot into sticks of equal size and shape, approximately 8cm long and 1cm square. Be sure to keep the offcuts for nibbles!

how to play

Stack the blocks of carrot in rows of three, with the first level pointing north–south and the next level on top pointing east–west. Continue this pattern until all carrots have been used.

Decide who is going first and then that person must use only one hand to try to remove a stick of carrot from anywhere within the tower and then place it on the top of the tower following the same pattern.

The game continues by taking it in turns to remove sticks of carrot and placing them on the top to build a higher tower.

The winner is the last person to place a carrot stick on the top before it falls over.

Once the tower has toppled, it's time to tuck in!

wriggly dinner

They'll really dig this down-to-earth sausage 'n' mash treat.

feeds 4

**1kg of potatoes, good for
    mashing**
**knob of butter and a splash of
    milk**
handful of Cheddar cheese
8 thin chipolata sausages
a few florets of broccoli
a squeeze of honey
Pre-heat your grill to a medium heat.

Take the potatoes, butter and milk
and make the mashed potato in your
favoured way. Grate the Cheddar
cheese into the mash according to
taste and mix it in well.

Grill the sausages for 10–12
minutes, turning frequently until
golden brown and cooked in the
middle, then remove from the heat.

Steam the broccoli florets for
3–4 minutes, until just cooked and
remove from the steamer.

To assemble your plate, spoon some
cheesy mash into individual bowls
or small side plates. Take the florets,
one at a time, and push each into
the mash, covering it completely.

Take two sausages and push them
inbetween the florets and into the
mash, just enough to hold them in
position.

Give your 'worms' some eyes by
sticking a thin slice of broccoli stem
in place with some honey and then
top with a dot of mash and a final
broccoli tip.

camp fire crackles

Parsnip and potato crisps to munch on.

parsnips
sweet potatoes
olive oil

Preheat the oven to 200C.

Using a Y-shaped vegetable peeler, remove the outer skin of both the parsnips and sweet potatoes and discard.

Continue peeling both vegetables in long thin strips.

Line a baking tray with baking parchment and lay the vegetable strips out ensuring they do not overlap. (You may need to do this in batches.)

Lightly brush the vegetable strips with olive oil and then bake in the oven for approximately 15–20 minutes, turning halfway through, until they are crisp and golden.

Remove from the oven and transfer to kitchen paper to dry away any excess oil.

Once cooled, your vegetable strips should be light and crispy. Loosely arrange the crisps into a camp fire stack and serve.

a dip in the ocean

Sail across the table with these guacamole boats.

makes 2 dips

1 ripe avocado, halved and
  stone removed
$\frac{1}{2}$ small red onion finely
  chopped
1 clove of garlic, grated
1 ripe tomato, chopped
juice of 1 lime
salt and black pepper, to taste
to serve
breadsticks
pitta bread

Carefully scoop out the avocado flesh into a bowl and mash well with a fork. Keep the shell.

Stir the onion, garlic, tomato and lime juice into the mashed avocado and season to taste.

Spoon the guacamole back into the empty avocado shells.

Slice open a pitta bread and then, from each slice, cut some sails by starting with a triangle shape and cutting a slight inward curve on two sides and curving the third side outwards.

Put the sails on a baking tray and pop under a preheated grill and toast for a few minutes, turning once until they are crisp.

Break a breadstick to about 8cm in length and stick it in the middle of your guacamole boat, then stand the pitta sails up in the mixture, leaning against the breadstick mast.

Use the pittas to dip into the guacamole when eating.

teepee treats

Set up camp round the party table and enjoy these crunchy filo pastries.

filo pastry sheets
melted butter, for brushing
milk chocolate

Preheat your oven to 180C.

Using some tin foil or baking parchment, make two or three cone shapes about 10cm high.

Take a sheet of filo pastry and cut it into 15cm squares.

Brush one sheet with melted butter and wrap around your cone shape tightly. Repeat this process with another 3 sheets, using melted butter to stick the sheets together and to hold all the edges down.

Stand your filo cones on a baking tray and bake in the oven for 4–5 minutes, until golden. Remove from the oven and allow them to cool.

Continue to make the filo cones until you have the amount you need.

Break the milk chocolate into a bowl over simmering water, stirring gently as it melts. Once done, very carefully place the melted chocolate into a piping bag.

Decorate them by piping an arched entrance at the bottom of one side and then a zigzag of chocolate near the top.

Pipe some long sticks of chocolate onto a baking sheet and chill until firm.

Trim the top of the cones and place some of the chocolate sticks inside, leaving them to poke proud of the top. Use any leftover chocolate shavings to build a campfire on the plate.

swamp jelly pots

Watch them sink their teeth into these funky jelly crocs.

1 packet of lime jelly
a few white marshmallows
a handful of grapes and raisins

Make the jelly according to the packet instructions and pour into small clear plastic cups or shot glasses and leave in the fridge to set.

Take the marshmallows and cut into strips. Then cut a serrated pattern along one edge to create the 'teeth'. Apply the marshmallows to the side of the cup (the cut edge of the marshmallow should stick to the side of the cup without too much effort).

To finish the crocodile, cut a grape into quarters. Make a slit into one of the cut edges of the grape and push half a raisin into the cavity. Repeat.

Sit the grape quarters onto the top of the jellies to create the eyes.

spuds-you-like

Fun baked jacket potato characters to liven any table.

makes 12 potatoes

12 small-/medium-sized baking
   potatoes
a little oil, for brushing
low-fat cream cheese
small jar of black olives
2 slices of ham

Preheat the oven to 200C.

Using a small circular cutter or a clean pen lid, carefully gouge out two 'eyes' near the top of each potato. Remove the eye piece leaving two holes about 5–10mm deep.

Brush the potatoes with a little oil and bake in a roasting tin for approximately 45–60 minutes, until crisp on the outside and fluffy in the middle. Remove the potatoes and allow them to cool to the touch.

Fill each 'eye socket' with a little cream cheese and then cut small circles from the olives for the pupils. Make a 'mouth' by taking a sharp knife and cutting a horizontal slit

below the eyes. Then take a small slice of ham, and poke inside the cavity, leaving a little sticking out to create a cheeky tongue.

funk it up...

To bring your potato people to life, use a selection of the following:

- red pepper slices
- cheese cubes
- cucumber slices
- broccoli florets
- herbs (parsley, chive or rosemary)
- cherry tomato
- sweetcorn

Take a few of your topping ingredients and use cream cheese to glue them into place. You can also make small holes in the surface of the potato and insert sticks, stalks and wedges of the above into place. Decorate them in the style of your choice and get the little ones involved too.

garden party

They won't be at snail's pace eating these.

cocktail sausages
375g ready-rolled puff pastry
a little Marmite
1 egg, beaten, to glaze
a few chives

Preheat the oven to 200C.

Roll out the puff pastry and cut strips about 4cm x 12cm and spread with Marmite.

At one end, place a cocktail sausage so that half of it is on the pastry and half is hanging over the end.

Fold the pastry over so that both edges touch and the sausage is held in place.

Spread a final thin layer of Marmite on top and then roll up from the non-sausage end until you reach the sausage and secure in place with a cocktail stick.

Brush with the beaten egg and place on a baking tray. Bake in the oven for 25 minutes until golden and crisp and the sausage is cooked through.

To decorate, trim some chives to 4cm and use a cocktail stick to poke two holes into the sausage 'head' and then insert the chives for the tentacles.

funk it up...

If Marmite is not your thing, then why not try a little tomato paste and finely grated cheese as your filling instead.

stars in their eyes

A healthy platter of stars and planets.

a selection of melons (such as
watermelon, cantaloupe,
Honeydew and Galia)

tools
melon baller
star- and moon-shaped cutters

Using a melon baller, scoop and cut various size melon balls to make your planets.

To create the Saturn ring, cut a slice of melon about 5mm thick and bigger than the melon ball. Cut out a large circle from the slice and then cut a smaller circle from the middle, the same size as the melon ball. Fit the ring of melon over the top.

Use the other shaped cutters or a sharp knife to create your solar system of stars and moons.

croak monsieur

These frog sandwiches will have them leaping for joy.

by Oscar Northeast, aged 7

makes 6 sandwiches

6 slices of brown bread
sandwich filling
ham slices
raisins
12 large green grapes
cucumber

Make up three rounds of sandwiches using the bread and preferred fillings. Cut two circles as large as you can from each sandwich.

Cut a grape in half and using a small knife, poke a hole in the front of each piece and then cut a small raisin in half and push each piece of raisin into the grape hole to make the pupils.

Take two slices of cucumber and cut each piece into a fan shape of three long toes.

Place the cucumber feet on your plate and then rest your round sandwich on top of the feet and put the eyes in place on top.

Finally, cut a long thin strip of ham and tuck one end into the sandwich and either roll the other end up to the mouth or extend the frog's tongue and place a raisin 'fly' on the tip.

flying saucers

Give them a close encounter with these simple snacks

makes 6 saucers

6 round crackers
cucumber
a few cherry tomatoes
cheese
a few black olives

To make one flying saucer, start with a single round cracker.

Cut a slice of cucumber and then using a small circular cutter, cut a circle of cucumber that fits on top of the cracker, but does not touch the edges

Cut a cherry tomato in half and place on top of the cucumber circle. Using a tiny cutter or sharp knife make some tiny discs of olive and stick these around the edge of the cherry tomato.

With a smaller circular cutter or clean pen lid, cut some little circles of cheese and set these around the edge of the cracker. Use some cucumber skin and add little dots on each small cheese circle for decoration.

To make the legs, take a wedge of cucumber and cut three pieces approximately 1cm square by 2.5cm in length.

Cut the base and top of each cucumber leg at an angle so that they tilt inwards when standing up. Sit the cracker on the top of the cucumber legs.

festive feast

A Yuletide spin on pizza.

large pizza base
1 jar of pizza topping sauce
Mozarella or feta cheese
red pepper
yellow pepper
a handful of spinach

Preheat the oven to 200C.

Take your pizza base and cut out a large Christmas-tree shape and then spread the base with some pizza topping sauce.

Using a small circular cutter, create some circles of red and yellow pepper.

Steam some spinach until just wilted and then decorate the tree with it and either some strips of Mozzarella or crumbled feta.

Finish the tree by adding the pepper, cut into the form of 'baubles' and a star for the top.

Bake in the oven for 10–15 minutes until the base is golden.

eye-scream

Have a chilling encounter with these fruity ice-cream treats.

handful of raspberries
icing sugar
handful of blueberries
1 tub of good quality vanilla ice-cream

Make a raspberry coulis by pushing a few raspberries through a sieve using the back of a spoon. Mix in a little icing sugar to sweeten the coulis and thicken it slightly.

Fill a small glass dish with a few blueberries and raspberries and then using a melon baller or small ice-cream scoop, place a round ball of ice cream on top of the dish.

Place a blueberry 'pupil' on top of the ice-cream ball and then, using a small spoon or syringe, drizzle the raspberry coulis over the eyeballs to create bloodshot veins.

yummy mummies

Pasta-embalmed meatball yumminess.

feeds 4

12 good quality meatballs
bag of dried tagliatelli
1 jar of tomato-based pasta
 sauce
black peppercorns
a little oil for frying

Using a shallow pan, lightly fry the meatballs for 10–12 minutes until golden brown and cooked through.

Meanwhile, fill a saucepan with cold water and bring to the boil. Add the tagliatelli and cook for 8–10 minutes according to packet instructions, until *al dente*.

When both the meatballs and pasta have cooked, allow them to cool slighty to the touch and then separate some strands of tagliatelli from the pan, take a meat ball and carefully wrap the pasta around the meatball like a bandage.

Repeat a couple more times until the meat ball cannot be seen. Poke a couple of peppercorns into the pasta for 'eyes'.

Heat some pasta sauce or passata in a pan and divide between 4 shallow bowls. Place 3 meatballs into each bowl of sauce and then warm through under a preheated medium grill.

This recipe was one of those moments where I'd thought I'd struck gold. The ink on my sketch of a pasta-wrapped meatball had hardly dried when I discovered a similar idea on the internet. It was an idea I had to share and so I must also urge you to visit the beautiful website I discovered, Gather and Nest, created and run by Cristine Roy. It is a great place to inspire parents.

flower power

These super-easy flower pot cakes will keep them in full bloom.

12 mini muffins in cases
1 chocolate Swiss roll cake
white chocolate buttons
milk chocolate buttons
raspberry jam
lollipop sticks

Take a muffin and carefully cut off the top of the muffin down to the paper case. Crumble up the cut-off muffin piece and then place back on top as 'soil'.

Use a sharp knife to cut slices from the Swiss roll about 1cm thick and lay flat on a surface.

Get some jam and stick the chocolate button 'petals' around the outside of the Swiss roll slice, adding an alternate colour button for the middle of the flower.

Using a lolly stick, carefully insert about 2cm of it into the slice of Swiss roll and then gently lift upright.

Insert the other end of the lolly stick in to the muffin pot and ensure it stands upright.

ca-tomato-pillar

They are going to *larva* this taste of Italy!

1 packet of cherry tomatoes
**1 pot of Mozzarella balls
   (pearls)**
a few black olives
handful of basil leaves
cocktail sticks (optional)

Build your caterpillars by taking
3 cherry tomatoes and two
Mozzarella balls and alternating
them on a plate. If you want to stop
them moving around, break a
cocktail stick into small pieces and
poke them into each piece to hold
them in place

To decorate the caterpillar face, use
a thin slice of Mozzarella and cut
2 small circles and then add a small
dot of olive skin for the pupil.

To make the mouth, cut a small
circle of olive skin and then using
the same size cutter, cut a crescent
moon shape from the small circle.
Press this against the tomato face
and it should stick. If not, then use a
little low-fat cream cheese to hold
the face features in place.

Finally, tuck a basil leaf under the
head of each caterpillar.

*Caution: If you have used cocktail
sticks to hold the caterpillars
together, ensure that these are
safely removed before eating.*

bear claw bites

Steps of fun all the way!

makes 20

350g/12oz plain flour, plus
   extra for rolling out
1 tsp bicarbonate of soda
2 tsp ground ginger
1 tsp ground cinnamon
125g/4¹/₂oz butter
175g/6oz light soft brown
   sugar
1 free-range egg
4 tbsp golden syrup
raisins

Sift together the flour, bicarbonate of soda, ginger and cinnamon and pour into the bowl of a food processor. Add the butter and blend until the mix looks like breadcrumbs. Stir in the sugar.

Lightly beat the egg and golden syrup together, add to the food processor and pulse until the mixture clumps together. Tip the dough out, knead briefly until smooth, wrap in clingfilm and leave to chill in the fridge for 15 minutes.

Preheat the oven to 180C. Line two baking trays with greaseproof paper.

Take a piece of dough mixture about the size of a walnut and roll into a short fat sausage shape and then bend in the middle to make a slight 'V' shape.

Take more dough and make two egg shapes about the size of a marble, and then make two more of them slightly larger.

On the outside of the 'V', press a small lip around the edge and using a dab of water, press the egg shapes onto the edge and against the V. Place the two larger egg shapes in the middle and the smaller ones on either side.

Once they are all fixed in place, use a small sharp knife to cut an opening in the front of each one and then cut a raisin lengthways in half and push it into the opening leaving enough sticking out for a 'claw'.

Transfer the tray carefully to the oven and bake for 12–15 minutes, or until lightly golden-brown. Leave on the tray for 10 minutes and then move to a wire rack to finish cooling.

chicken pops

Cluckingly good savoury sensations.

makes 10

250g minced chicken or
   uncooked chicken breast
4 tbsp roughly cut breadcrumbs
1 tbsp ketchup
$^1/_2$ tsp dried oregano
1 egg, beaten
plain flour
fine breadcrumbs
to decorate
10 wooden sticks
red pepper
carrot
black olives
low-fat cream cheese or low-fat
   mayonnaise

Preheat the oven to 190C and line a baking sheet with parchment paper.

Mix the chicken mince, rough breadcrumbs, ketchup and oregano into a bowl by hand (if using chicken breast, pulse in a blender first).

Make the chicken balls. Fill a large bowl with cold water, put the beaten egg, flour and the fine breadcrumbs into separate shallow dishes. Dip your hands into the water first and

then roll the chicken mixture into balls the size of walnuts (the water stops the chicken sticking to your hands). Next, roll the chicken into the flour, then the egg and finally the breadcrumbs. Continue rolling the chicken in a ball motion to remove the excess breadcrumbs and then place on the baking sheet. Bake for about 30 minutes until crisp and golden all over (cut into a spare one to check that they're cooked through). Leave to cool slightly.

While the chicken is cooking, prepare the decoration by cutting two small triangles of carrot for each 'mouth' and a three-pointed red pepper 'crown' for the top of the 'head'.

When the chicken is cool enough to handle, make a small hole on the top using a knife and push in the red pepper crown. Make another hole in the front of the chicken face and push the carrot in place to form an open beak.

Two dots of cream cheese or mayonnaise topped with small circles of olive will make the perfect 'eyes'.

funky games

Now they *can* play with their food!

**bowl of wholegrain cereal
squares**
icing sugar
**black and yellow food
colouring**

piping bag and small nozzle

Divide some icing sugar between three bowls and add a little water to each to mix into a paste. Add a dash of black food colouring to one of the bowls to achieve a jet-black colour; add a pin-head amount of yellow colouring to another bowl to achieve a pale yellow colour. Leave the third bowl as just the icing sugar and water paste.

Divide the cereal squares in half.

To make the **dominoes**, take one half of the cereal squares and, using a small paint brush, paint one side of each square with the black icing. Put onto a plate and chill in the fridge until the icing is set. When the dominoes are at least touch-dry, put some of the white icing into a piping bag and, using a small nozzle, pipe the spots into place. Do random selections of numbers between zero (leave blank) and six at either end of each domino. The children can then match up the numbers like a game of dominoes.

To make the **letter tiles**, take the remaining cereal squares and, using a small paint brush. paint one side of each square with the pale yellow icing. Put onto a plate and chill in the fridge until the icing is set. When the tiles are at least touch-dry, put some of the black icing into a clean piping bag and write a selection of letters, one onto each tile. When these have dried the children can have fun creating words.

cracking treat
Fool them with these sweet boiled eggs!

makes 12 eggs

for the meringue
1 egg white
pinch of salt
50g castor sugar
for the filling
1 ripe mango, peeled, de-stoned
200g of low-fat Greek yoghurt
spoonful of honey
1 tsp of arrowroot or cornflour
for the soldiers
250g gingerbread dough
   (see page 63 for recipe)

Preheat your oven to 150C and line a baking sheet with parchment paper.

Place the egg white and salt in a bowl and beat until fluffy. Gradually beat in the sugar until it is glossy and white and forms stiff peaks. Spoon out a tablespoon of mixture and push it off the spoon onto the baking sheet with your finger. The more dome-shaped and higher they are the more they will resemble egg shells. Shape your domes by dipping a finger into cold water and smoothing down any peaks. Alternatively, fill a piping bag and pipe out some domes straight onto the baking sheet.

Bake in the oven for 1 hour until cooked and crisp on the top. Remove and leave to cool completely.

To make the filling, sweeten the yoghurt by mixing in a spoonful of honey. Spoon the mixture into egg cups up to the rim and chill in the fridge.

Chop and purée the mango flesh with a blender. Place in a saucepan on the hob and add a teaspoon of arrowroot or corn flour. Heat gently, stirring occasionally until it thickens. Remove from the heat and allow to cool.

Remove the egg cups from the fridge and use a teaspoon to remove a little of the yoghurt mixture from the centre. Spoon the mango 'yolk' into this 'well'.

To make the soldiers, roll out your gingerbread dough to a thickness of 5mm and cut out lots of rectangles approximately 8cm x 2cm. Place onto a baking sheet and bake in a 180C-preheated oven for 12 minutes until golden. Remove from the oven and allow them to cool.

Top each egg cup with a meringue and serve with 2–3 soldiers for dunking.

arctic delights

A polar expedition worth the trek!

by Izzy Northeast, aged 9

makes 12 bears

4 packets of white chocolate buttons
packet of desiccated coconut
12 strawberries
a few squares of plain chocolate

Set aside 24 white chocolate buttons for the 'ears' and melt the rest of the chocolate buttons in a glass bowl either over simmering water or in a microwave.

Get a shallow dish and pour enough coconut in to cover the base.

When the melted chocolate has cooled a little, push a fork or small skewer into the stalk end of a strawberry and dip it into the chocolate, turning to coat it all over. Then quickly roll the chocolate-covered strawberry in the coconut, making sure that all the chocolate is covered and that the coconut sticks and holds in place. Tap the strawberry gently to remove any excess coconut and place on a plate.

Repeat with the rest of the strawberries (you may have to warm the chocolate up a few times if it starts to firm up). Once all of the strawberries are covered in the coconut, put the plate into the fridge until the chocolate has set.

To decorate the polar bear face, melt a few squares of plain chocolate and spoon the cooled melted chocolate into a piping bag. Squeeze out two dots for the eyes and then a round triangle shape for the nose.

To finish off, cut two slits into the strawberry behind the eyes on the top of the head. Insert a white chocolate button into each slit for the ears.

blooming marvellous

Pretty mini flower-shaped sandwiches.

bread slices
variety of sandwich fillings
to decorate
a selection of:
cucumber slices
red and yellow pepper
tomato slices
carrots slices
sweet corn
cress
equipment
flower-shaped cutter, circular
   cutters, apple corer and
   sharp knife

Make up enough sandwiches for your party and then, allowing one sandwich per child, cut one or two flower shapes from each sandwich. If you don't have a flower-shaped cookie cutter then start with a circle and working around the edge, trim five small 'V' shapes to leave you with the flower shape. You could round off the edges with a clean pair of scissors.

Using a smaller circular cutter or apple corer, remove a circle from the centre of the top layer of each sandwich, so you can see the filling through the hole.

Fill each hole with a variety of topping ingredients to decorate the inner flower circle, combining tomato and cress stems or using sweet corn on top of a tuna sandwich.

funk it up...

To create a 'meadow' of flowers, take a large foil platter and turn it upside-down to create a curved hill and then cover with leafy lettuce.

Cover the platter in your array of flower sandwiches and finish off with a few sprigs of cress, parsley or chives as blades of grass.

up, up and away

Sandwiches they won't want to let go of.

makes 8 balloons

4 slices of wholemeal bread
low-fat cream cheese
carrot
various colourful toppings like:
cucumber
cheddar slices
smoked salmon
red and yellow pepper

First cut the oval balloon shapes from your slices of bread (cut around a small glass using a sharp knife, extending one end into a more oval 'point'). You should be able to get two balloon shapes from each slice of bread. Repeat this process until you have 8 balloons. These are 'open' sandwiches, so you'll need just one slice of bread from which to cut the balloon shape.

Spread each balloon with some low-fat cream cheese and then top with a variety of different sandwich toppings to get a colourful selection.

Trim any over-hang of topping with a sharp knife or clean pair of scissors.

To make the balloon string, take a carrot and peel a long thin strip from it using a vegetable peeler. Trim the carrot strip with a knife until it is the width of a matchstick. Alternatively, use a zester and peel a couple of lengths of carrot.

Place all your balloon sandwiches on a platter and tuck the carrot string underneath.

funky tip...

Cut your carrot strings first and soak them in a bowl of cold water while you make the balloon sandwiches. The strips of carrot will be more flexible after soaking and easier to curve.

snow shake

A winter wonderland drink.

**vanilla ice cream or
mint ice cream
glass of milk or natural
yoghurt
green food colouring
(optional)
desiccated coconut
honey**

Start by decorating the glass and then leaving it to chill. To do this, squeeze a blob of honey on a plate and, with a thin paintbrush, paint a snowflake shape onto the outside of the glass. Then paint a thin line of honey around the lip of the glass.

On a separate plate spread a layer of desiccated coconut out and dip the lip of glass in the coconut ensuring it sticks all the way around. Pick up the rest of the coconut with your fingers and sprinkle it onto the snowflake shape you painted, gently tapping the glass to allow the loose pieces to fall off. Once your glass decoration is finished, pop it in the fridge to harden the honey and set the coconut.

Put the ice cream and milk into a blender and whizz until smooth. To get a slightly green colour, add a couple of drops of green food colouring and mix in. As an alternative, you could use mint ice-cream instead of vanilla, this will give a green colour without the need for extra colouring.

Slowly pour in the ice cream milkshake so it fills the glass and covers the snowflakes. These should now be visible against the green coloured drink.

thanks for *funky lunch* It's not often you get to thank your children for being stubborn, but without the grumbling of a 4-year-old boy on a sunny day in May, this whole chapter in my life would have drifted past unnoticed.

To Izzy and Oscar, thank you for eating what I put in front of you, and tasting things at least once, you are my inspiration and the reason why *Funky Lunch* works. To my wife Lisa, who never complains when she finds only half a carrot and a few skinned cucumbers left in the fridge and for allowing me to spend an entire family holiday chatting on my phone and laptop to the world's press.

To my unofficial PR mentor, Kelly Davies, whose off-the-cuff remark at the outset planted that first seed and for her enthusiastic tweeting which led me to Beth Murray, a complete stranger at the time, who on the promise of a sandwich placed me firmly in the media spotlight and started *Funky Lunch* on this rollercoaster ride. I still owe her that sandwich! Thank you ladies.

Huge appreciation goes to the team at Absolute Press for spotting the potential of *Funky Lunch* and believing in its concept. To Matt Inwood, whose tireless photography and design has captured the essence of this book perfectly and to the Inwood family for allowing me to commandeer their kitchen in the pursuit of sandwich excellence, thank you.

Finally, a special thanks to my friends and family whose encouragement and questioning of my sanity made me even more determined to succeed. To the hundreds and thousands of followers online, the blog writers, the tweeters, the Facebook devotees and everyone who has helped turn a simple idea into an amazing journey... I hope you enjoy this book.

---

thanks for *funky party* It's that part of the book where I am happy to take a step back and allow others to shine.

First up is Mr Matt Inwood of Absolute Press, the man with a thousand job roles, but only one job title and the driving force behind this book. My mentor, my timekeeper and my 2am e-mail buddy – and I thought I worked hard! I can't thank you enough.

To the rest of the team at Absolute Press and Bloomsbury Publishing who have given me yet another amazing chapter in my life: thank you.

A recipe book is just pages of ideas and words until you put it in the hands of some very talented people. To Gen and Jason: your understanding of this project was second to none and to work with you both has been a huge pleasure and great learning experience. Thank you.

To my wife, Lisa, and the two brightest lights in my life, Izzy and Oscar: thank you for tasting some random-looking recipe attempts and letting me lock myself away at the weekends to work on the book. I think you finally understand the phrase, 'Do not disturb'!

To Mum and Dad: thank you for your guidance and support over the years. I hope I continue to make you proud no matter how crazy this journey becomes.

To my special *Funky Lunch* fan club: you are a select group of ladies who have been my playground mums, my sounding board, my loud hailers, my supporters and my friends. Thank you Mrs P, Stacey, TC, Lu, Suze, Katie, Sarah and Clare.

And, finally, to the rest of my family, my friends, the Facebook and Twitter followers: your support and continued feedback helps to keep me moving *Funky Lunch* forward, and for that reason alone, I thank you.